Robert J. Chute

The Centennial Photographic Diary

A guide to photography, a guide to the Centennial, and a memorandum book

Robert J. Chute

The Centennial Photographic Diary
A guide to photography, a guide to the Centennial, and a memorandum book

ISBN/EAN: 9783337315948

Printed in Europe, USA, Canada, Australia, Japan

Cover: Foto ©Lupo / pixelio.de

More available books at **www.hansebooks.com**

PHOTOGRAPHIC HALL, CENTENNIAL EXHIBITION, 1876, PHILADELPHIA.

CENTENNIAL Photographic Diary.

A GUIDE TO PHOTOGRAPHY,
A GUIDE TO THE CENTENNIAL, AND
A MEMORANDUM BOOK.

By ROBERT J. CHUTE.

CONTENTS.

	PAGE
Rates of Postage,	4
Places of Interest in Philadelphia,	5
Railroad Depots and Ticket Offices,	6
Calendar,	from 7 to 28
Local Photographic Societies,	31
Items of Photographic History,	32
Photographic Processes,	36
The Negative Bath,	40
The Developer,	44
Collodion,	47
Varnishes,	47
Retouching Varnish,	48
Printing and Toning,	51
Mr. Marston's Process,	51
Mr. Hearn's Process,	52
Collodio-chloride for Porcelain Printing. By CHAS. EVANS,	59
Emulsion Process,	60
Photographic Hints,	63
Executive Officers of the United States Centennial Commission,	68
The Centennial Buildings,	71
Photographic Hall,	79
Directions for Exhibitors,	83
Important to Visitors,	84
Regulations for Admission to the Centennial Grounds,	84
Admission Tickets for Exhibitors and Employees,	88
Admission Tickets for the Public,	92
Hotel Charges,	96
N. P. A. Convention,	96
Map of Philadelphia,	97

Entered according to Act of Congress, in the year 1876, by BENERMAN & WILSON, in the office of the Librarian of Congress, at Washington, D. C.

SHERMAN & CO., PRINTERS, PHILADELPHIA.

PREFACE.

IN preparing this little work, I have had in view a threefold purpose: first, to supply visiting photographers to the Centennial Exhibition with such information as would be helpful to them in making the best use of their time, and deriving the greatest possible benefit from what they may see and hear in connection with the great show; second, to furnish brief, but comprehensive, formulæ for the principal photographic processes, which having been proved reliable, may help many to improvement in their work; and thirdly, to furnish a memorandum book, in which incidents, processes, statistics, expenses, etc., may be noted; the blank leaves being interspersed with the printed pages, this may be done in matters relating to photography or the Centennial, in connection with its appropriate subject.

Portions of this work have been condensed from the Public Ledger, the Public Ledger Almanac, and from some of the Centennial Guide-Books which have been published; I have been careful to have all information and every statement reliable.

R. J. C.

RATES OF POSTAGE.

Letters to any part of the United States or the Dominion of Canada, each half ounce, 3 cents.

Drop letters, where delivered by carrier, each half ounce, 2 cents; where there is no carrier, 1 cent.

Registered letters, 10 cents in addition to regular postage.

Books, circulars, transient newspapers, merchandise, etc., in packages not exceeding four pounds, for each ounce, or fraction thereof, 1 cent.

MONEY ORDERS IN THE UNITED STATES.—Orders not exceeding $10, 5 cents; $10 to $20, 10 cents; $20 to $30, 15 cents; $30 to $40, 20 cents; $40 to $50, 25 cents.

To Canada the rates are just four times the above.

POSTAGE TO FOREIGN COUNTRIES.—Letters not exceeding one-half ounce, to Austria,* Australia *via* San Francisco, Belgium,* France, German States *via* North German Union,* Great Britain and Ireland,* Holland, Italy *via* England,* Norway and Sweden,* Portugal *via* Southampton,* Russia *via* England,* Shanghai *via* San Francisco, Spain, Switzerland,* Syria, Turkey, etc., *via* England,* and West Indies, each 5 cents. Newspapers 2 cents.

Letters to Brazil, Japan *via* San Francisco, and Liberia,* each, 15 cents. Newspapers, to the first, 3 cents; to the two last, 4 cents.

Letters to Chili, Bolivia, Ecuador, and Peru, 17 cents. East Indies *via* San Francisco, 10 cents; Mexico, 1 cents.

* Prepayment optional.

PLACES OF INTEREST IN PHILADELPHIA.

ACADEMY OF FINE ARTS, Broad Street and Cherry, above Arch.—Admission, 25 cents.

ACADEMY OF NATURAL SCIENCES, Broad Street, below Chestnut.—Open Tuesdays and Fridays, P.M. Admission, 10 cents. New hall, S. W. corner Nineteenth and Race Streets.

BLIND ASYLUM, Twentieth and Race Streets.—Concerts Wednesdays, P.M. Admission, 15 cents.

CUSTOM HOUSE, Chestnut Street, below Fifth.

FRANKLIN INSTITUTE, Seventh Street, above Chestnut.

FAIRMOUNT PARK, 2991 acres, on the banks of the Schuylkill and Wissahickon.—Contains the Centennial Grounds. From central parts of the city, take cars going north or west.

GIRARD COLLEGE, Ridge Avenue, above Nineteenth Street.—Take Ridge Avenue cars or yellow cars on Eighth Street. Get tickets at *Ledger* Office.

INSANE HOSPITAL (KIRKBRIDE'S), Haverford Avenue, West Philadelphia.—Take Market Street cars.

INDEPENDENCE HALL, Chestnut Street, below Sixth.—Open from 9 A.M to 4 P.M. Tickets for admission to the steeple may be had of the superintendent.

MASONIC TEMPLE, Broad Street, below Arch.—Visitors admitted by card from resident members of the Order, on Thursdays, from 10 A.M. to 2 P.M. Cards of admission can also be procured at the *Ledger* Office.

MERCANTILE LIBRARY, Tenth Street, above Chestnut.

NATIONAL MUSEUM, Independence Hall.—Open from 9 A.M. to 3 P.M. Free.

PHILADELPHIA LIBRARY (founded by Benjamin Franklin), Fifth Street, below Chestnut.

PENNSYLVANIA HISTORICAL SOCIETY, No. 820 Spruce Street.

FAIRMOUNT WATER-WORKS, in the Old Park, east side of the Schuylkill River.—Open daily to visitors. Take Arch or Vine Street cars.

ZOOLOGICAL GARDENS, Fairmount Park.—Take cars on Walnut, Market, Arch, and Vine Streets, and Girard Avenue.

RAILROAD DEPOTS AND TICKET OFFICES.

PENNSYLVANIA RAILROAD.—Routes East and West. Depot, Thirty-first and Market Streets, West Philadelphia. Ticket Offices—838 Chestnut Street; S. E. corner Broad and Chestnut Streets; 116 Market Street; and at Depot.

PHILADELPHIA AND READING RAILROAD.—*Main Line—* Depots—Thirteenth and Callowhill Streets, and on Lansdowne Drive, near the Centennial Buildings. *Germantown and Norristown Branch—*Depot, Ninth and Green Streets. Ticket Offices—838 Chestnut Street; 317 Arch Street; 624 and 732 Chestnut Street; and at Depots.

NORTH PENNSYLVANIA RAILROAD.—Depot, Berks and American Streets. Ticket Offices—Fifth and Chestnut Streets; 732 Chestnut Street; and at Depot.

PHILADELPHIA, WILMINGTON AND BALTIMORE RAILROAD.—Depot, Broad and Washington Avenue. Ticket Offices, 700 and 838 Chestnut Street.

CAMDEN AND ATLANTIC RAILROAD.—From foot of Vine Street. Depot, Camden. Ticket Offices—838 Chestnut Street; S. E. corner Broad and Chestnut Streets; and foot of Vine Street.

WEST JERSEY RAILROAD.—From foot of Market Street. Ticket Offices—116 Market Street; 838 Chestnut Street; S. E. corner Broad and Chestnut Streets; and foot of Market Street.

PHILADELPHIA AND BALTIMORE CENTRAL.—Depot, Broad and Washington Avenue.

WEST CHESTER AND PHILADELPHIA RAILROAD.—Depot, Thirty-first and Chestnut Streets, West Philadelphia.

First Month,]   **JANUARY.**   [1876.

MOON'S PHASES.
	d. h. m.		d. h. m.
First Quarter..	4 0 23 A.M.	Last Quarter.. 18	3 48 A.M.
Full Moon......	11 1 22 A.M.	New Moon...... 26	8 41 A.M.

Month	Week		Sun Rises A.M. h. m.	Sun Sets P.M. h. m.
1	S	Emancipation, 1863.	7 23	4 45
2	S	*First Centennial Sunday.*	7 23	4 46
3	M	No negative baths to warm in 1776.	7 23	4 46
4	T	Newton born, 1642.	7 23	4 47
5	W	Chicago Photo. Association.	7 23	4 48
6	T	Philadelphia Photo. Society.	7 23	4 49
7	F	Photo. Art Society, Pacific. Boston Photo. Association.	7 23	4 50
8	S	Pay every week.	7 23	4 51
9	S	*Sweet day of rest.*	7 23	4 52
10	M	Warm the developer.	7 23	4 53
11	T	Pennsylvania Photo. Association.	7 23	4 54
12	W	John Hancock born, 1737.	7 22	4 55
13	T	Use a focusing glass.	7 22	4 56
14	F	Do not dip the plate too quick.	7 22	4 57
15	S	Fill all orders when promised.	7 21	4 58
16	S	*A change of thought rests the mind.*	7 21	5 0
17	M	Franklin born, 1706.	7 20	5 1
18	T	The Centennial work progresses.	7 20	5 2
19	W	James Watt born, 1736.	7 19	5 3
20	T	Use the long winter evenings	7 19	5 4
21	F	To study the principles	7 18	5 5
22	S	And art of Photography.	7 17	5 6
23	S	*The Sabbath was made for man.*	7 17	5 8
24	M	About this time	7 16	5 9
25	T	Begin to do the	7 15	5 10
26	W	Very best work you can.	7 15	5 11
27	T	If the collodion	7 14	5 13
28	F	Is too thick,	7 13	5 14
29	S	Thin with ether.	7 12	5 15
30	S	*A good day for head-rest.*	7 11	5 16
31	M	Fulfill all promises.	7 10	5 17

In the northern sections of our country cold snaps are in order this month, and water-pipes should be looked after. Wrapping exposed portions with woollen cloths is a preventive, but the surest is to shut off the water in the cellar, leaving the faucets open above. Keep all chemicals that will be affected by the cold where they will remain warm during the night.

Second Month.] **FEBRUARY.** [1876

MOON'S PHASES.
  d. h. m.   d. h. m.
First Quarter... 2 8 52 P.M. | Last Quarter.. 16 11 55 P.M.
Full Moon........ 9 0 46 P.M. | New Moon..... 23 1 19 A.M.

Month	Week		Sun Rises A.M. h. m.	Sun Sets P.M. h. m.
1	T	Washington elected President, 1779.	7 10	5 19
2	W	Chicago Photo. Association.	7 9	5 20
3	T	Philadelphia Photo. Society.	7 8	5 21
4	F	Boston Photo. Association.	7 7	5 22
5	S	Glacés require practice.	7 6	5 23
6	S	*Remember the seventh day.*	7 5	5 24
7	M	Charles Dickens born, 1812.	7 4	5 26
8	T	Early to work fills the orders.	7 2	5 27
9	W	William Henry Harrison born, 1773.	7 1	5 28
10	T	Keep your bath covered.	7 0	5 29
11	F	A foul Friday	6 59	5 31
12	S	Abraham Lincoln born, 1809.	6 58	5 32
13	S	*Brings a fair Sunday.*	6 57	5 33
14	M	St. Valentine never	6 55	5 34
15	T	Sat for his photograph.	6 54	5 35
16	W	Different conditions in the negative or	6 53	5 37
17	T	Printing departments, require different	6 52	5 38
18	F	Peace with England, 1815. [formulæ.	6 50	5 39
19	S	Stamp your proofs.	6 49	5 40
20	S	*Chemicals rest.*	6 48	5 41
21	M	Albumenize your glass. (See page 39.)	6 46	5 42
22	T	George Washington born, 1732.	6 45	5 43
23	W	G. W. did not sit	6 43	5 45
24	T	For his photograph in 1776.	6 42	5 46
25	F	Study art rules,	6 40	5 47
26	S	All pictures will help you.	6 39	5 48
27	S	*Longfellow born, 1807.*	6 37	5 49
28	M	When the bath shows	6 36	5 50
29	T	Alcohol markings, boil it.	6 34	5 51

The coldest weather of the winter is usually experienced this month. It is said to be very beneficial to a bath to set it out at night and let it freeze. There is no danger of the bottle or dish breaking, as it will not freeze solid. But do not do this unless you have another bath to work with in the morning, as damage might result from placing the bottle near the stove to warm it in a hurry. If obliged to operate in the morning while the room is cold, let the plate be in the bath longer, and move it up and down while coating.

MEMORANDA.

MEMORANDA.

Third Month,]   **MARCH.**   **[1876.**

Month	Week	MOON'S PHASES.		Sun Rises. A.M.	Sun Sets. P.M.
		First Quarter.. 3 4 47 A.M. Last Quarter.. 17 8 23 P.M.			
		Full Moon...... 10 1 11 A.M. New Moon..... 25 3 11 P.M.			
1	W	Chicago Photo. Association.		6 33	5 53
2	T	Philadelphia Photo. Society.		6 31	5 54
3	F	Photo. Art Society, Pacific.		6 30	5 55
4	S	Inauguration of President.		6 28	5 56
5	S	*Boston massacre*, 1770.		6 27	5 57
6	M	Michael Angelo born, 1474.		6 25	5 58
7	T	Herschel born, 1792.		6 24	5 59
8	W	An acid bath works slow.		6 22	6 0
9	T	German Photo. Association, New York.		6 21	6 1
10	F	Look out for breezes.		6 19	6 2
11	S	Study up for the Centennial.		6 17	6 3
12	S	*"Let us have peace."*		6 16	6 4
13	M	A weak bath will		6 14	6 6
14	T	Show pinholes.		6 13	6 7
15	W	Andrew Jackson born, 1767.		6 11	6 8
16	T	James Madison born, 1751.		6 9	6 9
17	F	Boston evacuated by British troops, 1776.		6 8	6 10
18	S	Do not fume with weak ammonia.		6 6	6 11
19	S	*"Righteousness exalteth a nation."*		6 4	6 12
20	M	John Tyler born, 1790.		6 3	6 13
21	T	Permanganate of potash		6 1	6 14
22	W	For disordered baths.		6 0	6 15
23	T	When prints are spotted		5 58	6 16
24	F	And weak in the shadows,		5 56	6 17
25	S	The silver bath is weak.		5 55	6 18
26	S	*Do not envy pleasant Sundays.*		5 53	6 19
27	M	Advance pay is safe.		5 52	6 20
28	T	Raphael born, 1483.		5 50	6 21
29	W	A wise man stores his mind with		5 48	6 22
30	T	Knowledge, but the foolish man		5 47	6 23
31	F	Wastes no money in books.		5 45	6 24

As the spring approaches the days are getting longer, and the gallery should be brushed up for the spring trade. This is one of the best months in the year for business. Look out the March winds do not blow your printing-frames off from the printing-shelf and spoil some of your good negatives. Get to printing early if you want to get off a good day's work. Print under ground glass or tissue paper, unless the negative be very intense.

Fourth Month.] APRIL. [1876

MOON'S PHASES

	d. h. m.		d. h. m.
First Quarter...	1 11 11 A.M.	Last Quarter...	16 3 36 P.M.
Full Moon.......	8 2 35 P.M.	New Moon......	24 2 2 A.M.
		First Quarter..	30 5 26 P.M.

Sun Rises. A.M. / Sun Sets. P.M.

Month. Week.			Sun Rises A.M.	Sun Sets P.M.
1	S	No trust.	5 43	6 23
2	S	*Thomas Jefferson born*, 1743.	5 42	6 24
3	M	Study works of art.	5 40	6 25
4	T	Photo. Sec., American Institute, N. Y.	5 39	6 26
5	W	Chicago Photo. Association.	5 37	6 28
6	T	Washington declared President, 1789.	5 36	6 30
7	F	Boston Photo. Association.	5 34	6 31
8	S	How about landscapes?	5 32	6 32
9	S	*Leave business at the gallery.*	5 31	6 33
10	M	Are your negatives sufficiently timed?	5 29	6 34
11	T	Pennsylvania Photo. Association.	5 28	6 35
12	W	Retouching cannot compensate	5 26	6 36
13	T	For bad lighting or under-timing.	5 25	6 37
14	F	Good Friday.	5 23	6 38
15	S	Lincoln died, 1865.	5 22	6 39
16	S	*Easter Sunday—Shakspeare born*, 1564.	5 20	6 40
17	M	Be sure the prints are washed	5 19	6 41
18	T	Free from silver before toning.	5 17	6 42
19	W	Battle of Lexington, Mass., 1775.	5 16	6 43
20	T	Napoleon III. born, 1808.	5 14	6 44
21	F	Pure distilled water is best	5 13	6 45
22	S	For all photo. chemicals.	5 12	6 46
23	S	*James Buchanan born*, 1791.	5 10	6 47
24	M	Long washing affects the	5 9	6 48
25	T	Brilliancy of the prints.	5 8	6 49
26	W	Short washing may cause fading.	5 6	6 50
27	T	President Ulysses S. Grant born, 1822.	5 5	6 51
28	F	Monroe born, 1758.	5 4	6 52
29	S	Do not put off till next week.	5 2	6 53
30	S	*Washington inaugurated*. 1789.	5 1	6 54

Now is the time to begin to get things together for out-door work. Those who expect to go into the field should see that their apparatus is in order. If you have heretofore been loading yourself with trappings for the wet process, this is the time to try some of the dry or emulsion processes, and see if you cannot go much more comfortably and with the ability to do much more work. A little practice now with dry plates may prepare you for successful field work later in the season.

MEMORANDA.

MEMORANDA.

Fifth Month.] **MAY.** [1876.

		MOON'S PHASES.		Sun Rises.	Sun Sets.
		d. h. m.	d. h. m.		
Month.	Week.	Full Moon...... 8 4 52 A.M. New Moon...... 23 10 25 A.M.		A.M.	P.M.
		Last Quarter... 16 8 26 A.M. First Quarter.. 30 0 47 A.M.		h. m.	h. m.
1	M	The Centennial opening draws near.		5 0	6 55
2	T	Photo. Section, American Institute, N. Y.		4 59	6 56
3	W	Chicago Photo. Association.		4 57	6 57
4	T	Philadelphia Photo. Society.		4 56	6 58
5	F	Boston Photo. Association.		4 55	6 59
6	S	Nearly all pictures contain art lessons.		4 54	6 59
7	S	*Millard Fillmore born*, 1800.		4 53	7 0
8	M	N. P. A. Convention met at St. Louis, 1872.		4 52	7 1
9	T	Will you be in Philadelphia to-morrow ?		4 51	7 2
10	W	Centennial Exhibition opens, 1876. Cont. Congress met in Philadelphia, 1775		4 50	7 3
11	T	Visit the Art Gallery.		4 49	7 4
12	F	Photographic Hall possesses		4 48	7 5
13	S	Great attractions for everybody.		4 47	7 6
14	S	*Is the Exhibition open to-day ?*		4 46	7 7
15	M	Do not go home till you		4 45	7 8
16	T	Have filled the blank leaves		4 44	7 9
17	W	With notes, hints,		4 43	7 10
18	T	Thoughts on art, suggested by		4 42	7 11
19	F	The beautiful pictures,		4 41	7 12
20	S	The magnificent sculpture,		4 40	7 12
21	S	And the improved processes		4 39	7 13
22	M	And formulæ that you may		4 38	7 14
23	T	Get from brother photographers.		4 38	7 15
24	W	Queen Victoria born, 1819.		4 37	7 16
25	T	If things do not work well		4 37	7 17
26	F	When you get home,		4 36	7 18
27	S	Refer to your Diary.		4 36	7 18
28	S	" *Rest, sweetly rest.*"		4 35	7 19
29	M	Patrick Henry born, 1763.		4 35	7 20
30	T	Weather getting warm.		4 34	7 21
31	W	Keep collodion cool.		4 34	7 21

In this delightful month the actinic rays are more active than at any other season, so that short exposures, both in doors and out, may be looked for. Remember, that for out-door work by the wet process you require a much heavier collodion than for the gallery. Collodion with from six to seven grains of iodide to the ounce will be found to give the most vigorous negatives.

Sixth Month,]   **JUNE.**   [1876.

MOON'S PHASES.
d. h. m.   d. h. m.
Full Moon...... 6 7 36 P.M. | New Moon...... 21 5 16 P.M.
Last Quarter... 14 10 13 P.M. | First Quarter.. 28 10 13 A.M.

Month	Week		Sun Rises A.M.	Sun Sets P.M.
1	T	First convention of N. P. A., Boston, 1869	4 31	7 22
2	F	Knights Templar parade, Phila., 1876. Photo. Art Society, Pacific.	4 33	7 23
3	S	Side and front light for sunken eyes.	4 33	7 23
4	S	"*Six days shalt thou labor.*"	4 33	7 24
5	M	Study to see the light and shade.	4 32	7 25
6	T	N. P. A. met at Philadelphia, 1871.	4 32	7 25
7	W	First American Congress. 1765. N. P. A. met in Cleveland, Ohio, 1870. Philadelphia, 1871.	4 32	7 26
8	T	Avoid too many lines	4 32	7 26
9	F	In one direction. [York, 1871.	4 32	7 27
10	S	Statue of Prof. Morse inaugurated in New	4 31	7 28
11	S	*Study the minister's face.*	4 31	7 28
12	M	Study all faces you see.	4 31	7 28
13	T	General Scott born, 1786.	4 31	7 29
14	W	Do not use a low side-light,	4 31	7 29
15	T	To get a well-lighted face,	4 31	7 30
16	F	A low top-light alone is better.	4 31	7 30
17	S	Battle of Bunker Hill, 1775.	4 31	7 30
18	S	"*Apples of gold in pictures of silver.*"	4 32	7 30
19	M	The night rate (nitrate) of silver	4 32	7 31
20	T	Is regulated by the day rate of gold.	4 32	7 31
21	W	Lines in portraiture	4 32	7 31
22	T	Are formed by the limbs	4 32	7 31
23	F	Of the sitter;	4 33	7 32
24	S	By folds of drapery;	4 33	7 32
25	S	*By accessories;*	4 33	7 32
26	M	By imaginary lines	4 33	7 32
27	T	Touching some of the	4 34	7 32
28	W	Principal points,	4 34	7 32
29	T	Such as the head and shoulders,	4 35	7 32
30	F	In connection with others in the picture.	4 35	7 32

Now the days are beginning to be warm. The sun will reach his highest northern altitude this month. Shades will be required on the skylight, if at any time. When the light is so situated that it can be screened upon the outside, it increases the comfort inside immensely during the warm weather, and at the same time gives a much more even and manageable light.

MEMORANDA.

MEMORANDA.

Seventh Month,] JULY. [1876.

Month	Week	MOON'S PHASES.	Sun Rises. A.M. h. m.	Sun Sets. P.M. h. m.
		Full Moon...... 6 10 37 A.M.	New Moon..... 20 11 52 P.M.		
		Last Quarter... 14 8 55 A.M.	First Quarter.. 27 10 18 P.M.		
1	S	Summer is upon us.	4 36	7 32
2	S	*Last Sunday in the century we celebrate.*	4 36	7 31
3	M	A great day in Philadelphia to-morrow.	4 37	7 31
4	T	THE 100TH ANNIVERSARY OF AMERICAN INDEPENDENCE.	4 37	7 31
5	W	Chicago Photo. Association.	4 38	7 31
6	T	German Photo. Society, New York.	4 38	7 31
7	F	Boston Photo. Association.	4 39	7 30
8	S	Ventilate the studio well.	4 40	7 30
9	S	*A warm heart and mind at peace will cause*	4 40	7 30
10	M	Columbus born, 1447. [*no perspiration.*	4 41	7 29
11	T	John Quincy Adams born, 1767.	4 41	7 29
12	W	When sitters perspire,	4 42	7 28
13	T	Keep cool yourself.	4 43	7 28
14	F	N. P. A. met at Chicago, 1874.	4 44	7 27
15	S	N. P. A met at St. Louis, 1873.	4 45	7 27
16	S	*Sir Joshua Reynolds born, 1823.*	4 46	7 26
17	M	Study Sir Joshua's	4 47	7 25
18	T	Lectures on art;	4 48	7 25
19	W	They will do you good.	4 49	7 24
20	T	German Photo. Society, New York.	4 49	7 23
21	F	Keep your printing-bath cool;	4 50	7 23
22	S	Otherwise the paper will turn yellow.	4 51	7 22
23	S	*Seek for truth.*	4 52	7 21
24	M	Let the plate be	4 53	7 20
25	T	In the bath five minutes.	4 54	7 19
26	W	Robert Fulton born, 1765.	4 55	7 19
27	T	Atlantic cable laid, 1866.	4 55	7 18
28	F	Art study is profitable.	4 56	7 17
29	S	All study is good.	4 57	7 16
30	S	*"Contentment is better than riches."*	4 58	7 15
31	M	Thick varnish can be thinned with alcohol	4 58	7 14

Open the windows and doors; ventilate the gallery well. Provide plenty of fans for customers; place cool water where they can help themselves. Keep the dark-room well ventilated, especially if it has a southern or roof exposure. Keep the ammonia bottle in a cool place. Collodion which is being used is easily kept cool by placing the bottles in a dish or pail of water.

Eighth **Month,**] AUGUST. [1876

MOON'S PHASES.

	d. h. m.		d. h. m.
Full Moon......	5 1 37 A.M.	New Moon......	19 7 25 A.M.
Last Quarter...	12 4 58 P.M.	First Quarter.	26 1 17 P.M.

Month	Week		Sun Rises. A. m.	Sun Sets. A. m.
1	T	Photo. Sec.. American Institute, N. Y.	4 59	7 1
2	W	Chicago Photo. Association.	5 0	7 1
3	T	Columbus sailed on his expedition, 1492.	5 1	7 1
4	F	Photo. Art Society, Pacific.	5 2	7 0
5	S	A calm day for out-door work.	5 3	7 0
6	S	"*Love thy neighbor as thyself.*"	5 4	7 0
7	M	Keep the bath well iodized.	5 5	7 6
8	T	Pennsylvania Photo. Association.	5 6	7 5
9	W	Save the silver drippings.	5 7	7 3
10	T	Daguerre died, 1851.	5 8	7 2
11	F	A pin in the dipper	5 9	7 1
12	S	Is better than spots on the negative.	5 10	7 0
13	**S**	*Truth in the Heart—Truth in Art.*	5 11	6 58
14	M	Printing invented, 1437.	5 12	6 57
15	T	A good light is better	5 13	6 56
16	W	Than a marble front.	5 14	6 54
17	T	A dirty gallery	5 15	6 54
18	F	Is like a bad picture—	5 16	6 52
19	S	Neither is attractive.	5 17	6 50
20	**S**	*Smiles are better than frowns.*	5 18	6 49
21	M	Negative bath, thirty-five grains;	5 18	6 47
22	T	Keep up its strength.	5 19	6 46
23	W	A good lens is better	5 20	6 44
24	T	Than a Brussels carpet.	5 21	6 43
25	F	A blue sky	5 22	6 42
26	S	Gives a slow light.	5 23	6 40
27	**S**	*The golden rule is good.*	5 24	6 38
28	M	A soft answer turns away	5 25	6 37
29	T	The wrath that might	5 26	6 36
30	W	Appear in the picture.	5 27	6 34
31	T	Make your sitters cheerful.	5 28	6 32

The printing bath must be kept cool if you would have your paper keep white after silvering. If the skylight becomes dusty wash it off, it will make a difference in the working of the light. If flies are troublesome while making sittings, stand near the sitter during exposure and keep them off with a fan. Look after the lenses this dry, dusty weather, and see that they are wiped clean every day. Use a soft chamois skin.

MEMORANDA.

MEMORANDA.

Ninth Month.] SEPTEMBER. [1876.

MOON'S PHASES.

	d. h. m.		d. h. m.
Full Moon......	3 4 12 P.M.	New Moon......	17 4 53 P.M.
Last Quarter...	10 11 29 P.M.	First Quarter..	25 7 2 A.M.

Month	Week		Sun Rises. A.M. h. m.	Sun Sets. P.M. h. m.
1	F	Boston Photo. Association.	5 28	6 31
2	S	Visit the Centennial.	5 29	6 29
3	S	*Good tones come from the church organ.*	5 30	6 28
4	M	Look for the cause of every trouble.	5 31	6 26
5	T	First American Congress met in Philadelphia, 1774.	5 32	6 24
6	W	Chicago Photo. Association.	5 33	6 23
7	T	When prints show a scum	5 34	6 21
8	F	In toning, it may be removed	5 35	6 20
9	S	With a piece of canton flannel.	5 36	6 18
10	S	*Who is my neighbor?*	5 37	6 16
11	M	Dust is an enemy.	5 37	6 15
12	T	Pennsylvania Photo. Association.	5 38	6 13
13	W	A good negative is better	5 39	6 11
14	T	Than a bushel of rejected prints.	5 40	6 10
15	F	All copying for enlargements	5 41	6 8
16	S	Is best done in direct sunlight.	5 42	6 6
17	**S**	" It is lawful to do good."	5 43	6 5
18	M	A low light works	5 44	6 3
19	T	Quicker than a high one.	5 45	6 1
20	W	Direct sunlight should be	5 46	6 0
21	T	Excluded from the operating-room.	5 47	5 58
22	F	Filter the varnish when dirty.	5 48	5 56
23	S	Rough the edges of glass before using.	5 49	5 55
24	**S**	*" Buy the truth and sell it not."*	5 50	5 53
25	M	A dozen good prints	5 51	5 52
26	T	Are better than a barrel	5 52	5 50
27	W	Of waste paper.	5 53	5 48
28	T	Weak silvering or short fuming	5 54	5 47
29	F	Produce alike—measley prints.	5 55	5 45
30	S	Cover all solutions at night.	5 56	5 44

Throughout a large portion of our country this is one of the most delightful months of the year. Often in the early part of September we have some of those beautiful days when all nature seems to be at rest. Lake or river reflects everything in its mirror-like surface; every leaf obeys the sweet influence of the calm and quiet repose that pervades the landscape. These are the days for outdoor photography.

Tenth Month,]   **OCTOBER.**   **[1876.**

MOON'S PHASES.

Full Moon...... 3 5 55 A.M. | New Moon..... 17 4 56 A.M.
Last Quarter... 10 5 19 A.M. | First Quarter.. 25 2 53 A.M.

Month	Week		Sun Rises A.M. h. m.	Sun Sets P.M. h. m.
1	S	To be good and true, is noble.	5 56	5 42
2	M	Pose every sitter carefully.	5 58	5 40
3	T	Photo Sec., American Institute, N. Y.	5 59	5 39
4	W	Battle of Germantown, 1777.	6 0	5 37
5	T	Philadelphia Photo. Society.	6 0	5 35
6	F	Photo. Art Society, Pacific.	6 2	5 34
7	S	Burning of Chicago, 1871.	6 3	5 32
8	S	"Keep thy heart with all diligence."	6 4	5 30
9	M	Look out for streaks.	6 5	5 29
10	T	Pennsylvania Photo. Association.	6 6	5 27
11	W	Neutralize the bath before boiling.	6 7	5 26
12	T	America discovered, 1492.	6 8	5 24
13	F	Babies require patience.	6 9	5 23
14	S	William Penn born, 1644.	6 10	5 21
15	S	Battle of Camden, 1776.	6 11	5 20
16	M	A clean plate is better	6 12	5 18
17	T	Than a peeled-off negative.	6 13	5 17
18	W	Exclude white light from the dark-room.	6 14	5 15
19	T	Cornwallis surrendered, 1781.	6 15	5 14
20	F	Profane words and a bad bath	6 17	5 13
21	S	Are usually found together.	6 18	5 11
22	S	In good deeds, let every day be Sunday.	6 19	5 10
23	M	To a thin face,	6 20	5 8
24	T	Give more front light.	6 21	5 7
25	W	For white hair,	6 22	5 6
26	T	Shade the top of the head.	6 23	5 4
27	F	Learn to see that nothing	6 24	5 3
28	S	Is out of place, before exposing.	6 25	5 2
29	S	Keep in the light.	6 27	5 1
30	M	John Adams born, 1735.	6 28	5 0
31	T	Always select the best view.	6 29	4 58

As the fall weather comes on, and rainy days are more frequent, improve the time in clearing up and cleaning out the dust of summer. Look after your apparatus on rainy days. If the plate-holder leaks, give it a thorough overhauling. Fill all the cracks and cover the wood-work (where it will not interfere) with melted paraffine. This is a most useful article, and may be employed as a protector and lubricator.

MEMORANDA.

MEMORANDA.

Eleventh Month,] **NOVEMBER.** [1876.

		MOON'S PHASES.	Sun Rises.	Sun Sets.
		d. h. m. d. h. m.	A.M.	P.M.
		Full Moon...... 1 6 30 P.M. New Moon... 15 7 47 P.M.	h. m.	h. m.
		Last Quarter.... 8 0 16 P.M. First Quarter.. 23 11 25 P.M.		
1	W	Chicago Photo. Association.	6 30	4 57
2	T	James K. Polk born, 1795.	6 31	4 56
3	F	Boston Photo. Association.	6 32	4 55
4	S	Make better work than yesterday.	6 34	4 54
5	**S**	*"Seek and ye shall find."* [low.	6 35	4 52
6	M	Do not work the camera too high or too	6 36	4 52
7	T	Photo. Sec., American Institute, N. Y.	6 37	4 50
8	W	Avoid hypo drippings on the floor.	6 38	4 49
9	T	Great fire in Boston, 1872.	6 39	4 48
10	F	Close of the Centennial Exhibition, 1876.	6 41	4 48
11	S	Have tanks for prints well washed.	6 42	4 47
12	**S**	*Thou shalt not covet thy neighbor's camera.*	6 43	4 46
13	M	Montreal captured by Americans, 1775.	6 44	4 45
14	T	Mozart born, 1719.	6 45	4 44
15	W	Do not let the bath get cold.	6 46	4 43
16	T	Destruction of tea in Boston harbor, 1773	6 47	4 42
17	F	Encourage your help to read	6 48	4 42
18	S	Something instructive, when not busy.	6 49	4 41
19	**S**	*"Learn to do good; cease to do evil."*	6 51	4 40
20	M	A cheerful operator	6 52	4 40
21	T	Is better than a sour sitter.	6 53	4 39
22	W	Expression is the key to truth.	6 54	4 38
23	T	Franklin Pierce born, 1804.	6 55	4 38
24	F	Zachray Taylor born, 1790.	6 57	4 37
25	S	Evacuation of New York by the British, 1783.	6 58	4 37
26	**S**	*What is truth?*	6 59	4 36
27	M	A fogging bath and a cross baby	7 0	4 36
28	T	Will try the spirit of any photographer.	7 1	4 36
29	W	How to make Collodio-chloride, see page 32.	7 2	4 35
30	T	Prepare for Christmas work.	7 3	4 35

"Things work fearfully slow!" Consult your neighbor, and you will find he has the same trouble. Some of these clear November days, with a blue sky and chilly atmosphere, not cold enough, perhaps, to put on the whole heating apparatus, are yet sufficiently cool to cause all this trouble of slow working, better fire up and keep everything warm. Begin to prepare for Christmas trade. Show new styles, new mounts, new frames, etc.

Twelfth Month,] DECEMBER. [1876.

```
              MOON'S PHASES.                   Sun    Sun
        d.  h.  m.              d.  h.  m.    Rises. Sets.
Full Moon..... 1  6  3 A.M. | New Moon..... 15  1  13 P.M.
Last Quarter.. 7  9 22 P.M. | First Quarter. 23  6  40 P.M.  A.M.  P.M.
                            | Full Moon..... 30  4  55 P.M.  h. m. h. m.
```

1	F	Photo. Art Society, Pacific.	7 44 4 35
2	S	Collodion, equal parts ether and alcohol.	7 54 4 34
3	**S**	"*Get wisdom, get understanding.*"	7 64 4 34
4	M	Washington's farewell, 1783.	7 74 4 34
5	T	Martin Van Buren born, 1782.	7 84 4 34
6	W	Chicago Photo. Association.	7 94 4 34
7	T	Philadelphia Photo. Society.	7 10 4 34
8	F	The long winter evenings	7 11 4 34
9	S	Afford time for study.	7 12 4 34
10	S	"*A good name is better than riches.*"	7 12 4 34
11	M	Do all work well.	7 13 4 34
12	T	Pennsylvania Photo. Association.	7 14 4 35
13	W	" Time lost is never regained."	7 15 4 35
14	T	Washington died, 1799.	7 15 4 35
15	F	A well finished picture	7 16 4 35
16	S	Makes a glad customer.	7 17 4 36
17	**S**	*Faith, hope, charity.*	7 18 4 36
18	M	Is a negative imperfect, spoil it.	7 18 4 36
19	T	Never let a poor print be mounted.	7 19 4 37
20	W	Pilgrims landed, 1620.	7 19 4 37
21	T	Keep all solutions	7 20 4 38
22	F	At a moderate temperature.	7 20 4 38
23	S	Prepayment is *sure pay*.	7 21 4 39
24	**S**	*Do not worry over unfinished work.*	7 21 4 40
25	M	Christmas—make the children happy.	7 21 4 41
26	T	Andrew Johnson born, 1808.	7 22 4 41
27	W	Renew your subscription to the *Philadelphia Photographer*.	7 22 4 42
28	T	Battle of Trenton, 1776.	7 22 4 43
29	F	Make better work now	7 23 4 44
30	S	Than you did a year ago.	7 23 4 44
31	**S**	*Good-bye*, 1876.—"*In God we trust.*"	7 23 4 44

Cold weather is likely to be upon many of us in earnest at this time. The printing bath will bear to be stronger by ten or twenty grains than in summer. If, however, all the apartments be well warmed, this is not so necessary. The dark-room especially should be kept at a temperature of from 65° to 70°. If you are hurried with holiday work, increase your force; it will pay.

MEMORANDA.

MEMORANDA

LOCAL PHOTOGRAPHIC SOCIETIES.

Photographic Society of Philadelphia.—J. C. BROWNE, *President;* ELLERSLIE WALLACE, *Secretary;* DR. CARL SEILER, *Corresponding Secretary.* Meets first Tuesday, monthly, at 520 Walnut Street.

Pennsylvania Photographic Association.—H. S. KELLER, *President;* CHARLES EVANS, *Secretary,* 814 Chestnut Street. Meets second Tuesday, at Mahan and Keller's, 1427 Ridge Avenue.

Photo-Section of the American Institute, New York.—H. J. NEWTON, *President;* OSCAR G. MASON, *Secretary,* Bellevue Hospital. Meets at the Institute, the first Tuesday in each month.

Boston Photographic Association.—BENJ. FRENCH, *President;* A. N. HARDY, *Secretary,* 22 Winter Street. Meets at the Studio of J. W. Black, on the first Friday.

Maryland Photographic Association, Baltimore.—N. H. BUSEY, *President;* G. O. BROWN, *Secretary.*

German Photographic Society of New York.—WILLIAM KURTZ, *President;* ERNEST KRUGER, *Corresponding Secretary,* 27 Avenue A. Meets at 64 & 66 East Fourth Street, every Thursday.

Chicago Photographic Association.—P. B. GREEN, *President;* O. F. WEAVER, *Secretary.* Meets at C. W. Stevens' "Great Central," 158 State St., on the first Wednesday of each month.

Photo-Art Society of the Pacific.—JACOB SHEW, *President;* GEO. B. REIMAN, *Secretary.* Meets at the galleries of the members, on the first Friday in each month.

Indiana Photographic Association.—J. PERRY ELLIOTT, *President;* D. O. ADAMS, *Secretary.* Meets on the first Wednesday of each month.

ITEMS OF PHOTOGRAPHIC HISTORY.

The Camera Obscura was invented by Giovanni Baptiste Porta, a Neapolitan physician, in the 16th century. He discovered that light passing through a small hole into a darkened chamber, conveyed a representation of objects outside. He applied a lens to the aperture, and — he had it!

In the early part of the eighteenth century Charles William Scheele discovered that chloride of silver spread on paper was speedily darkened in the blue rays of light, while the red rays produced little or no change.

The first published account of an attempt to produce pictures by the decomposing powers of light was given by Mr. Wedgwood, in June, 1802, it being "a method of copying paintings upon glass, and making profiles by the agency of light upon nitrate of silver; with observations by H. Davy."

In 1814 M. Niepce, of Chalons, turned his attention to the chemical agency of light, and discovered its peculiar property in altering the solubility of many resinous substances.

In 1824 Daguerre began a series of experiments in a direction very similar to that of M. Niepce.

In 1826 Daguerre and Niepce became acquainted with each other.

On the 14th of December, 1829, M. Niepce and M. Daguerre entered into partnership for the purpose of prosecuting their photographic researches together. In communicating his process to Daguerre, on the 5th of December, 1829, M. Niepce prefaced it with this statement: "The discovery which I have made, and to which

MEMORANDA.

MEMORANDA.

I gave the name of Heliography, consists in producing spontaneously by the action of light, with gradation of tints from black to white, the images received by the camera obscura."

In July, 1833, M. Niepce died, and a new agreement was entered into between his son, M. Isidore Niepce, and Daguerre.

In January, 1839, the discovery of M. Daguerre was reported and specimens shown to the scientific world of Paris.

January 31st, 1839, Mr. H. Fox Talbot, an English gentleman of philosophic attainments, communicated to the Royal Society of England, "Some account of the art of Photogenic, or the process by which natural objects may be made to delineate themselves without the aid of the artist's pencil." Three weeks later, February 21st, he communicated the process in detail.

On the 19th of August, 1839, Daguerre's process, having been communicated to the French government, in consideration of an annual pension of 6000 francs (which was afterwards increased to 10,000 francs) to Daguerre, and 4000 francs to Niepce, Jr., was made public.

In October 1839, Mr. Walcott of New York, took the first Daguerreotype portrait.

Prof. Draper, of the University of New York, is said to be entitled to the credit of having first applied photography to portraiture from life. M. Fizeau invented the method of gilding the Daguerreotype; M. Claudet discovered how to take it instantaneously; and Mr. F. Scott Archer, an English gentleman, discovered the collodion process, which has now entirely superseded the Daguerreotype.

PHOTOGRAPHIC PROCESSES.

UNDER this head I propose to give some of the most approved formulæ and methods of working, culled from the writings of others as well as from my own experience. The first step in the negative process is the selection and preparation of the glass. Here is where the *boy* begins, and whether it be to rub or albumenize, he looks upon it as the lowest down and hardest part of the work. Suitable glass is now manufactured expressly for photography, and may be had of any dealer in photographic goods. Before the plates are used it is well to roughen the edges by taking two at a time and drawing the corners across each other. Another precaution which saves a great deal of valuable time, when it is most valuable, is to try each plate in the holder, or in a form of the same size, as every photographer has doubtless experienced the annoyance of finding a prepared plate when taken from the bath too large for the holder. New glass should be placed for a few hours, or over night in a bath of diluted nitric acid—eight or ten ounces of commercial nitric acid to one gallon of water. Some use a portion of sulphuric acid. This may be an improvement.

While the glass is preparing, thus far, we will attend to another preliminary process. The use of albumen as a means of producing a clean surface has now become so general, both for wet and dry plates, that I unhesitatingly recommend it for all practical work. The method of preparing the albumen is of some importance, and may materially affect the quality of the resulting negative. That given by Mr. John Carbutt, in

PHOTOGRAPHIC DIARY.

MEMORANDA.

MEMORANDA.

Mosaics for 1876, is so reasonable and of such manifest advantage that I will give it here and recommend its use. He says:

"I prepare it in the following manner: Open twelve fresh hen's eggs; place the whites in a shallow dish, take forty minims glacial acetic acid, add to half an ounce of water, with a strip of glass stir the whites, dropping the dilute acid in, continue stirring leisurely until the coagulum you will see forming spreads through, and is incorporated with the before clear but viscid albumen; it will occupy for this quantity about a minute to a minute and a half. Now leave for about an hour, when you will find the fibrous matter collected at the surface; pour the whole on to a damp cloth or flannel placed over a funnel, when the clear albumen will pass through, and the slimy mucus will remain behind; to clear the albumen add one fluid drachm of ammonia, keep corked up, and you will have albumen purified and ready for use in any part of photography you may wish to apply it. For preparing negative glass, I use one part to twenty parts water for dry-plate photography. No other method of preparing albumen can equal it."

This albumen may be dried, and in this way is much more easily kept or transported. Mr. Carbutt has proved it to be perfectly soluble and readily prepared.

When the albumen is required for use it should be filtered. For this purpose take a tuft of cotton, wet it with alcohol, then wash with water till the alcohol is displaced, and without squeezing or matting the cotton together, drop it in the neck of the funnel; it may be gently pressed down to keep it in place when the albumen is poured in. To prevent bubbles, take a piece of clean twine, wet it thoroughly, and let it pass through the neck of the funnel before the filter is put in; this twine reaching to the bottom of the wide-mouth bottle or graduate glass, acts as a conductor for the albumen, and effectually prevents the formation of bubbles. A little albumen should be poured into the filter first and allowed to run to waste, to displace the water. The albumen being ready, the plates are taken from the acid, thoroughly washed under the tap, over which has been tied two thicknesses of stout muslin or canton flannel, and while wet they are flowed with the albumen. This should be done carefully, so that none may get on the under side of the plate and yet with sufficient volume to cover it well, and drive off all the water upon the surface. Let the surplus flow into the sink, and place the plate on a clean rack to dry; while the plates are drying be very careful to protect them from dust. Always coat the concave side of the glass.

When glass is required for immediate use without time for all this preliminary preparation, select some of the cleanest plates, and apply old or new collodion (the first is the best), rubbing it briskly with a pad of Joseph's paper or bleached canton flannel, after which apply a little alcohol, and polish with another pad. This will give clean plates for use at once, without any washing; but it would be hardly practicable where a large number were being used.

The next in the order of preparation is

THE NEGATIVE BATH.

If distilled water can be procured from a reliable chemist, it is best for all chemical purposes; but avoid any drippings from greasy machinery. Any water may be made sufficiently pure by dissolving in it a few grains of nitrate of silver, and setting it in the sun

MEMORANDA.

MEMORANDA.

until it becomes clear. This can only be used, however, for silver solutions:

Pure water,	14 ounces.
Nitrate of silver,	1 ounce.
Iodide of potassium,	1 or 2 grains.

After dissolving the silver, dissolve the potassium in a little water and add to the solution; shake well and filter. This bath may be used at once with a ripe collodion, but will be more reliable after adding a drop or two of C. P. nitric acid and letting it stand an hour or two.

Various plans are pursued for keeping the negative bath in order:

Mr. W. H. Sherman, of Milwaukee, one of our most advanced men, especially in the chemical department, gives his process in *Mosaics* for 1876. He adds to a sick bath, after it has been filtered and brought to its original strength with silver, about one grain of cyanide of potassium to each ounce of silver nitrate, shake well, let settle, decant the clear liquid, and filter the residue. Now add three fluid drachms of acetic acid, No. 8, to each quart of solution. Next neutralize with bicarbonate of soda, and set in the sun until it settles clear; then filter again. Finally, add nitric acid (C. P.) until all tendency to fog is removed. When more bath is required, make up the new as usual and proceed to treat it as just described, and then add to the old. This, it is claimed, keeps the bath in a ripe and excellent working condition.

Mr. Charles Waldack, whose reputation as author, teacher, and first-class photographer stands high on both sides of the Atlantic, treats his bath with chloride of silver. His plan is so simple, and I have no doubt effectual, that I do not hesitate to recommend its use.

This remedy is based on the theory that a precipitate will absorb and carry down the organic matter in the bath. To a disordered bath, he recommends to add of a solution of common salt, or chloride of ammonium, a quantity sufficient to produce an abundant precipitate. A few crystals of nitrate of silver may be added to make up for the loss. The solution is well shaken and the chloride of silver permitted to settle, when the clear part may be filtered and is ready for use. The precipitate may remain in the bottle and the bath be added every night, drawing it off clear every morning. After a time the precipitate has taken up all the organic matter it can hold, and must then be thrown into the waste. The ether and alcohol are expelled by boiling, as usual.

THE DEVELOPER.

In preparing the iron developer, either the plain or double sulphate may be used. I prefer the latter, and recommend as follows:

Double sulphate of iron and ammonia,	4 ounces.
Water,	1 quart.

This gives a stock solution of sixty grains to the ounce. When required for use, filter, double its bulk with water, and add one ounce of acetic acid, No. 8, to every six or eight ounces of developer. It is well, in the dark-room, to have a bottle of the developer prepared, full strength, to assist in bringing up short exposures and for children's sittings. It saves developer to use a small graduate, or wide-mouthed bottle, to flow the plates with—one holding a little more than enough solution to develop the negative is best.

MEMORANDA.

MEMORANDA.

COLLODION.

Make a solution of equal parts of ether and alcohol; to each ounce of this add five grains of iodide of ammonium and two grains of bromide of potassium. Dissolve the salts in a very little water and add to the ether and alcohol. Shake well, and, after the resulting precipitate is settled, filter through paper, and it is ready for use. This is a sensitized solution and will keep any length of time. Collodion from this should only be prepared in sufficient quantity to last a few days. About six grains of cotton to the ounce should be used, and by filtering is ready for use at once. A better collodion is made, however, by mixing the new with a sample of old.

A good keeping collodion may be made as follows:

Ether and alcohol,	equal parts.
Iodide ammonium,	3 grains to ounce.
Iodide cadmium,	2 grains to ounce.
Bromide cadmium,	2 grains to ounce.

These salts may all be dissolved in the ether and alcohol, or a better way is to dissolve the excitants in the alcohol, then add the cotton, let it become thoroughly soaked, and finally add the ether. This collodion should be set aside, in a cool, dark place, for several days, as it will require to ripen before being used. Mixing this with the formula first given will make a very fine collodion.

VARNISHES.

Captain Abney's formulæ:

Alcohol,	16 ounces.
*Unbleached lac,	2 ounces.
Sandarac,	2 ounces.
Canada balsam,	1 drachm.
Oil of thyme or lavender,	1 ounce.

---

* Bleached lac absorbs moisture and tends to make the varnish crack.

Amber varnish, which is applied to a cold plate, is made as follows:

No. 1.—Amber in fine powder.. 1 ounce.
Chloroform, 16 ounces.

Or,

No. 2.—Amber, . 1 ounce.
Benzole, . 16 ounces.

Heat the amber in a closed vessel till it begins to soften, when it will dissolve readily in the solvents.

Mr. William H. Tipton's formula:

Gum sandarac, ... 12 ounces.
White turpentine (gum), . 12 ounces.
Alcohol, 95 per cent., . 1 gallon.

RETOUCHING VARNISHES.

Herr Jean Eppel gives the following:

Oil of turpentine (rectified), . 2 parts.
Common resin, ... 1 part.

When dissolved it is applied to the already varnished negative by means of a soft rag stretched over the finger. If the rag sticks to the film in rubbing, the varnish is too thick, and should be diluted with the oil of turpentine. When dry, this varnish will take any pencil, either hard or soft.

The following is from the *Year Book* for 1876:

Ether, $3\frac{1}{2}$ ounces.
Shellac, . 15 grains.
Sandarac, . . . 90 grains.
Mastic (in drops), . . . 90 grains.

After the above are in solution, add about two and one-half drachms of benzole. Use cold, and it will give a malt film. If the grain is not fine enough, add a little more benzole.

MEMORANDA.

MEMORANDA.

PRINTING AND TONING.

In this department I prefer to let the practical men give the best formulæ. The following processes were prepared expressly for this work. Mr. David Marston is printer for Mr. Wm. H. Rhoads, and Mr. Charles W. Hearn, proprietor of Hearn's Printing Institute; both of Philadelphia. These gentlemen have printed many of the embellishments for the *Philadelphia Photographer*, and their work is sufficiently well known to commend to all the following brief and simple formulæ, which are given as their latest and best.

MR. MARSTON'S PROCESS.

Silver solution, thirty grains (hydrometer test); to every twelve ounces add one and one-half ounces of alcohol, and three grains of bicarbonate of soda,—the bicarbonate of soda is used as a preventive of measles,—float the paper one minute. On removing a sheet from the bath, commence at the end that was last down, and after lifting it clear of the dish reverse it and hang it up by the corner that first touched the solution. After draining a few moments I thoroughly dry it by the aid of a gas furnace, and then fume fifteen minutes. It may be as well for me to state here that I print under ground glass. Before toning the prints are soaked in a tray of water ten minutes, then washed in running water for fifteen minutes, and finally treated to a solution of about two ounces of salt in a gallon of water; from this they are taken direct to the toning solution, which is as follows: Acetate of soda, eighty grains; water, one quart. This is prepared about twenty-four hours before using. About half an hour before using, add two grains of chloride of gold neutralized with bicarbonate of soda. After the prints are toned, fix in the following solution:

Hyposulphite of soda, eight ounces; water, one gallon; at about the same temperature as the room, and then transfer them to the washing tank. I find fifteen minutes in the fixing solution sufficient.

To keep the bath in order, every day after using the solution (if it be clear) add a few grains of bicarbonate of soda, shake it up well, and set it out in the sunlight for the remainder of the day. When the bath becomes disordered or foul, I pour it into the evaporating dish and boil it down to about one-third its original bulk; after it cools off filter and add the necessary amount of water to reduce it to strength and sun for several days, and then treat as a new solution. I have followed this plan for several years and it has never failed me.

The prints are all cut out before toning.

My wash tank is of wood, with the supply pipe running around the top, the water being introduced in fine jets about two inches apart. The stand pipe is about four (4) inches high, with three (3) small holes in the lower end, so as to come on a line with the bottom of the tank of sufficient capacity to carry off about one-half the waste water, and insuring a more thorough washing of the prints, three hours being sufficient therefor.

The prints are taken out of the tank and laid on ordinary blotting pads to absorb the surplus water, and mounted while still damp with starch paste.

MR. HEARN'S PROCESS.

Silver **Solution.**—This bath must vary according to the temperature of both the room in which it is used, as well as that where the printing is done. If the negatives are printed in a warm room in the winter, then no stronger bath is required than during the summer months.

I will below give baths for summer use as well as for

MEMORANDA.

MEMORANDA.

winter, advising those who may try to use or follow them to modify their strength, etc., according to the salting of the brand of paper used.

SUMMER BATH.

Nitrate of silver, ... 40 grains.
Nitrate of ammonium, ... 20 grains.
Distilled water, ... 1 ounce.

Slightly alkaline with liquid ammonia.

This bath, as well as the one below, will work excellently with "Morgan's H. Extra" and "Clemons' New" paper, but for the "cross-sword" brand of German paper imported by Shwarze & Valk, Philadelphia, the nitrate of ammonium should be left out.

WINTER BATH.

Nitrate of Silver, ... 50 to 60 grains.
Nitrate of ammonia, ... 30 to 40 grains.
Distilled water, ... 1 ounce.

For summer use float from twenty to forty-five seconds for single paper; for double paper from forty to seventy-five seconds.

For winter use float the paper thirty-five to sixty-five seconds for single paper (the time varying so widely on account of the uncertainties of the temperature of the room, etc.), while for double paper the time of floating should vary from forty-five to eighty-five seconds.

The sooner the prints are placed in the toning bath, after they are removed from the printing frame, the better will be the finished results. When ready to commence washing and toning operations, make up an acetic acid bath of the strength of one ounce of the acid to the gallon of water, and place the prints therein, a few at a time. When they have changed to a pretty red color, remove them immediately, and place them in a tank of fresh running water, which tank should be used for this purpose alone. After they have been washing about fifteen minutes, care being exercised to keep them constantly separated from each other, they are ready to be placed in the toning bath.

At the best galleries the toner has an assistant whose business it is to acidify prints for the toning bath, and at no first-class place are there ever more than 50 or 75 prints acidified at a time. It only takes about ten minutes to acidify and place to washing, and hence the prints are not damaged by *too long* washing before toning.

Printing.—Good prints can be best obtained from printing under one or more tissue papers.

TONING BATH.

Acetate soda,	60 grains.
Chloride sodium (common salt),	60 grains.
Chloride gold,	4 grains.
Water,	32 ounces.

Make slightly alkaline with bicarbonate of soda before toning. Tone a little purple.

FIXING BATH.

Hypo. soda (saturated solution),	1 ounce.
Water,	7 ounces.
Bicarbonate soda (saturated solution),	¼ ounce.

Hints.—Always keep the light away from the prints after they are once removed from the printing frames, as the delicate printing of the whites is injured even by the exposure of a few seconds in a tolerably dark room. Keep dark curtains around the place where you change the paper in the frames.

If you are engaged upon extra fine work, do not try to see how many can be obtained in a day, but how nice they can be. Remember slow printing is (except in very intense negatives) always the best.

MEMORANDA.

MEMORANDA.

Keep the negatives well dusted, and when pinholes are to be touched out, try to make the touched out places print as if there was no defect there. This saves spotting, after mounting, which never leaves the print as nice as it would be if the brush had never been applied. I always consider the use of the brush on the print that is to be burnished, to be a decided injury, and detracts from the beauty of the results, however well it may have been done. As far as possible try to make the mounted print require nothing but burnishing, then you are sure of a fine finish and a perfect surface, which cannot be had when spotting has to be done.

(Written for the Centennial Photographic Diary.)
COLLODIO-CHLORIDE FOR PORCELAIN PRINTING.
BY CHARLES EVANS.

PHOTOGRAPHERS who have had little experience in making collodio-chloride, fail in forming the chloride of silver in the collodion without precipitation. The following formulæ will give little or no precipitation of chloride of silver, but keep in suspension, which is the success of all chloride of silver emulsions. There are several formulas for making collodio-chloride, some containing little chloride of silver, and others more; my object has been to give to the photographer, a simple and successful formula, which, if followed with care, will not fail to give good results.

Formula.—Make plain collodion as follows: Ether, twelve ounces; alcohol, six ounces; cotton, one hundred grains. Now take twenty grains citric acid, thirty-two grains chloride of strontium, and dissolve by grinding in two ounces of alcohol; after all is dissolved add to the plain collodion and shake well. Now take one hundred and twenty grains of nitrate of silver, grind very fine, and add four ounces of alcohol; grind together until the alcohol will take up no more silver, then add water, two or three drops at a time, grinding well after each addition, until all the silver is dissolved; this is now to be added to the collodion containing the acid and strontium; the silver must be introduced in small quantities at a time, and well shaken after each addition, until all is added. If successful the collodion should have a light opal color, inclining to a pink, when looked at by transmitted light. This is the stock collodion; when wanted for use take from two to four ounces, and for each ounce add one drop of aqua ammonia, shake well, and in a short time it is ready for use.

Albumenize the plates with albumen one part, water two parts; if intended to keep add two or three drops of ammonia. Before coating the plates with the collodion they must be thoroughly dried with a gentle heat to expel the moisture from the albumen, also a gentle heat applied to the plates before printing.

Tone in a weak bath containing very little gold and a few grains of salt. Slow toning gives the best results.

Fix in hyposulphite of soda one ounce, water twelve ounces, for five minutes, and wash thoroughly.

EMULSION PROCESS.

The following is Mr. Newton's Emulsion Process with some modifications by Mr. A. F. Chase, as published in the *Philadelphia Photographer* for March:

Ether,	6 ounces.
Atwood's alcohol,	4 ounces.
Bromide of cadmium,	120 grains.
Parys' special cotton,	75 grains.

Dissolve the bromide in the alcohol, add the cotton next, and lastly the ether; take from the above three ounces, and add fifty-four grains of fused nitrate of silver

MEMORANDA.

MEMORANDA.

finely pulverized and dissolved in alcohol by boiling. Let stand eight or ten hours, and then add twelve grains of chloride of cobalt dissolved in one-half ounce of alcohol.

The preservative (organifier) is prepared as follows:

 Roasted and pulverized coffee, ... ½ ounce.
 Atwood's alcohol, ... 1 ounce.

Digest for about a week and filter; add fifteen or twenty drops to the emulsion and it is ready to use. Develop with a three-grain solution of pyrogallic acid and water till all details are visible, when a few drops from either of the following vials of ammonia solution completes the intensity:

 Water, ... ¾ ounce.
 Ammonia (concentrated), ... ¼ ounce.

In one vial put five grains of bromide of ammonium, and in the other fifteen grains. If the exposure has been too long use from the fifteen-grain vial, or mix to suit the case.

The above process has proved very successful in the hands of some of our best amateur and professional photographers, and I trust, from its simplicity, that many others may be induced to give it a fair trial.

PHOTOGRAPHIC HINTS.

Fix negatives in a saturated solution of hyposulphate of soda.

Use a focusing-glass, if you would save your eyes and have uniformly sharp negatives.

Make the light comfortable for the sitter, if you would secure a natural expression.

When the bath is cold warm the plate before developing; use a warm developer also.

The development should proceed till a slight deposit is on the deepest shadows, then all detail will be secured.

Float the paper by laying one corner of the sheet on the bath first instead of the middle.

A very cold toning bath may work too slow, and a hot one too fast. There is a medium that is best.

The study of the rules and principles of art, as applied to photography, is one of the surest means of improvement.

Dip a plate slowly; never plunge it into the bath. Draw it from the bath quickly, and drain it before placing in the holder.

Should the holder not save the drippings from the plates properly, place strips of blotting-paper along the lower edge of the plate, to absorb the solution.

To be up with the times, the photographer should read everything he can get hold of relating to the art, and not hesitate to put in practice or try any new formulæ or suggestion. This is the way to improve.

A lamp or small gas jet should be in such position that the plate may be held between the light and the eye, so that every stage of the development may be carefully watched.

In coating a plate, flow the collodion steadily and bring the plate into a perpendicular position, rocking it gently till the collodion begins to set, then hold it horizontally till ready for the bath; this will avoid lines in the direction of the draining.

MEMORANDA.

MEMORANDA.

Clips of card-board, made of pieces two inches long and one inch wide, and folded together, are capital for handling plates as they come from the bath. They protect the fingers, while they absorb and save the silver.

To redevelop a negative, wash well, then flow with a twenty-grain solution of silver, flowing on and off two or three times, and flow again with the developer. If sufficient intensity is not gained in this way, fix and wash thoroughly; then repeat the redeveloping till the required intensity is obtained.

To reduce intensity in an old negative or new one,— if old remove the varnish with alcohol—flow the plate with a weak solution of iodine in alcohol, wash it well, and then flow with a rather strong solution of cyanide of potassium. Should one application not reduce sufficiently, repeat the operation.

In developing, do not pour on the plate any more than enough to cover it freely. Hold the plate still, if your time and light have been correct, and the negative will develop with all its gradations and detail. If there be signs of flatness, rock the plate; if too much contrast appears, wash the plate quickly with a fresh flow of developer.

A good collodion for copying engravings or line subjects, where strong contrasts are required, may be hastily prepared by adding to some good portrait collodion about one-third its bulk of old red collodion. Flow this so as to get as thick a film as possible. Leave in the bath only long enough to dispose of the greasy lines, give a short exposure in a strong light, and a negative with brilliant contrast will be the result.

EXECUTIVE OFFICERS

OF THE

United States Centennial Commission.

President,
JOSEPH R. HAWLEY, Connecticut.

Director-General,
ALFRED T. GOSHORN, Ohio.

President of Executive Committee,
DANIEL J. MORRELL, Pennsylvania.

Secretary,
JOHN L. CAMPBELL, Indiana.

Solicitor,
JOHN L. SHOEMAKER, Esq., Philadelphia.

Assistant Secretaries,
MEYER ASCH, DORSEY GARDNER.

Executive Committee,

DANIEL J. MORRELL, *Penna.*; ALFRED T. GOSHORN, *Ohio*; N. M. BECKWITH, *New York*; ALEXANDER R. BOTELER, *W. Virginia*; RICHARD MCCORMICK, *Arizona*; JOHN LYNCH, *Louisiana*; CHAS. P. KIMBALL, *Maine*; SAMUEL F. PHILLIPS, *North Carolina*; GEO. B. LORING, *Massachusetts*; FREDERICK W. MATHEWS, *Illinois*; WM. PHIPPS BLAKE, *Connecticut*; JAMES E. DEXTER, *District of Columbia*; J. T. BERNARD, *Florida*.

MEMORANDA.

MEMORANDA.

THE CENTENNIAL BUILDINGS.*

THE MAIN BUILDING.

This vast edifice is 1880 feet long and 464 feet wide, covering an area of more than 20 acres. It is built mainly of iron and glass, the roof being boarded and covered with tin, and so lighted that every part will be equally desirable for exhibition purposes. The four central towers are each 48 feet square, and being divided into stories, which communicate by easy stairs, rise to the height of 120 feet, and afford magnificent views both of the grand interior and the buildings and grounds outside. This immense structure was built by Mr. R. J. Dobbins, and cost $1,600,000.

MEMORIAL HALL.

The grand Memorial Hall or Art Gallery, is the gem of the whole Centennial group. Its magnificent proportions, and almost faultless symmetry, claim the admiration of all who see it. It is 365 feet in length, 210 feet in width, and 59 feet in height, surmounted by a dome over the centre, which rises to a height of 150 feet from the ground.

The main portion of the building is constructed of granite, iron and glass, and is thoroughly fire-proof. The dome is built of iron and glass, and is surmounted by a colossal statue of Columbia. The four corners of the base of the dome support figures representing the four quarters of the globe.

The interior is divided into a grand entrance hall 82 x 60 feet, and 53 feet high; a central gallery beneath

---

* Fine lithographic engravings of eight of the principal buildings will be found on the margins of the map of Philadelphia, which accompanies this work.

the dome 82 feet square; and two other galleries leading east and west, each 88 x 98 feet, and 35 feet high. These three central halls form a vast gallery 287 feet long, and capable of holding 8000 persons. Beyond these, on either end, is a smaller gallery 28 x 98 feet. Besides these there are a number of studios and small exhibition rooms. The large galleries are all lighted from above.

This building will doubtless be the most attractive part of the whole exhibition, especially for those who have a taste for art. It should be the resort, above all others, for photographers, who may be greatly benefited by a careful study of the grand works of art there collected.

Memorial Hall is elevated on a terrace which is ascended at each entrance by a broad flight of thirteen steps. It was built by the State of Pennsylvania as a permanent Centennial Memorial, at a cost of $1,500,000, which sum was appropriated by the State for that purpose. The great demand for space in the art department soon overran this building, and rendered it necessary that the Centennial Commission should erect a temporary structure of about equal capacity, thus doubling the extent of the art exhibition, and accommodating treasures from every land.

MACHINERY HALL.

Machinery Hall is situated on a line with the Main building, and separated from it by Belmont Avenue. It is 1402 feet long by 360 feet wide, and covers nearly fourteen acres. In the centre, on the south side, is an annex 208 x 210 feet, and containing a tank 60 x 106 feet, which is filled with water ten feet deep. At the south end of the tank is a beautiful waterfall 35 feet high by 40 feet wide, which is supplied with water by pumps

MEMORANDA.

MEMORANDA.

on exhibition. Ten thousand feet of shafting conveys the motive power, which is furnished by a single Corliss engine of 1300 horse-power.

The Bureau of Machinery will prove a most interesting department of the exhibition, and one in which American skill and enterprise will be amply demonstrated.

AGRICULTURAL HALL.

This building is of singularly original design, and well adapted to the purpose for which it is intended. It consists of a main section 826 feet long, 100 feet wide, and 75 feet high. This is crossed by a central transept of the same height and width, and two subdividing transepts each 70 feet high and 80 feet wide, and 540 feet long, the whole covering an area of 9½ acres. This structure is of the gothic style, each section forming an arch, which springs directly from the ground. This plan of construction does away with any interior supports, and gives the whole inclosed space entirely free from obstruction. In the centre of the building, a tower surmounted by a dome, rises to the height of 130 feet, and each exterior corner is supported by a smaller tower of similar design.

As Agriculture is the basis of all material prosperity, this department will command as well the attention of the philosopher as of the humblest tiller of the soil who may visit the Centennial.

HORTICULTURAL HALL.

This unique but magnificent building is so suggestive of the oriental that it is difficult to think of it as of American design and construction. It is to be a permanent building, and is built of glass, iron, brick and stone, is 385 feet long by 193 feet wide, and covers one and a quarter acres. Its exterior beauty is only equalled by its interior magnificence. The central portion of the structure forms one vast conservatory 230 feet long, 80 feet wide and 55 feet high. Nine ornamental fountains adorn the conservatory and add to its freshness and beauty. On the north and south sides of this principal hall are four forcing-houses, for the propagation of young plants, each 100 feet long by 30 feet wide, covered with curved roofs of iron and glass. The grounds connected with the Horticultural department consist of about 40 acres, which are laid out into beautiful gardens, and filled with the rarest and most attractive plants. The Horticultural department promises to be one of bewitching beauty and transcendent loveliness.

In addition to the five principal buildings of the Centennial group, three others will be erected by the Commission, viz., the Judges' Hall, the Women's Pavilion, and Photographic Hall. Besides these there will be a great number of others, erected by the various governments who will participate in the exhibition, by a number of the States of our union, by corporations and by individuals.

Among the more important of these are the Government Building erected by the United States Government; the English, the Brazilian, the Japanese buildings and the Centennial Photographic Company's Studio.

An immense restaurant is being erected which will accommodate 5000 persons, and furnish meals at the same price as are paid in the city proper.

From the foregoing some estimate may be formed of the extent and magnitude of this Centennial enterprise. The exhibition space alone, provided for in the buildings, comprises about 75 acres; and applications have been so numerous and extensive that in most cases the applicants have been awarded but half the space applied for, and yet all this vast area is full to overflowing, so

MEMORANDA.

MEMORANDA.

that in some cases, as in that of the Art department, the Centennial authorities have felt obliged to extend by erecting additional buildings.

The grounds set apart for the exhibition comprise 236 acres, most charmingly located on the west bank of the Schuylkill River, and being beautifully laid out in walks, gardens, lakes, fountains, etc., will form such a world of beauty in itself as has never been witnessed in this country, and such as the present generation will not be likely to see again.

PHOTOGRAPHIC HALL.*

Photographic Hall, and the Photographic Exhibit, will form one of the principal centres of attraction for photographers from all parts of the world. It is situated a little east of Memorial Hall, in a commanding and very accessible position, being near the north entrance to the Main Building.

The dimensions are 258 feet long by 107 feet wide. The interior is arranged with twenty-eight screens, for hanging pictures, four of which are 19 feet long, and twenty-four are 24 feet long, each. These screens together with the wall space, furnish 19,080 square feet of surface for the Photographic Exhibit.

Mr. John Carbutt of Philadelphia, has been appointed superintendent of Photographic Hall, and, a better selection could not have been made. He is a gentleman thoroughly conversant with almost every department of our art, is well known both in this country and in Europe, and there is every reason to believe that in his official capacity there, he will receive the confidence and respect of photographers everywhere to the same extent that these have always been accorded him in his individual and business relations.

---

* See Frontispiece.

That the display in Photographic Hall surpasses anything of the kind ever seen before, there can be no doubt. Here are to be seen views and portraits from Japan, illustrating the scenery and the people of that far off country; views from Australia, 3 feet by 5 feet in size, the largest photographs in the world from direct negatives; a splendid collection of views and reproductions in carbon, by M. Adolph Braun, of Dornach, France—these will be especially worthy of study, particularly the reproductions of works of art by the old masters; the wonderful photochromic pictures, or photographs printed in colors, by M. Leon Vidal of Paris, will also excite interest and admiration. Besides these novelties, the exhibits from Germany, France, England and our own country, will be found to contain many beautiful works which will be well worth revisiting and studying again and again. This is to be the golden opportunity for American photographers; and all who come should come, not only to feast the senses, to enjoy and admire, but come prepared to *learn*, come with minds open to the reception of every new truth, and ready to grasp, and, if possible, to appropriate every new thought. This six months of the Centennial Exhibition ought to be as productive of improvement, of culture in art, and a general awakening to a sense of the importance and capabilities of photography as any six years we have even known since its discovery.

The Centennial Photographic Installation Co., Chas. A. Wilson & Co., managers, acting under authority from the Bureau of Art Administration, will attend to the hanging, decorating, insuring, selling when desired, and repacking and shipping of photographic exhibits for those who may not find it convenient to attend to it personally. Their charges are moderate.

MEMORANDA.

MEMORANDA.

DIRECTIONS FOR EXHIBITORS.

The following, from the "General Directions for Exhibitors from the United States," may be of interest to photographers:

The Commission will take precautions for the safe preservation of all objects in the exhibition, but it will in no way be responsible for damage or loss of any kind, or for accidents by fire or otherwise, however originating.

Favorable facilities will be arranged by which exhibitors may insure their own goods.

Exhibitors may employ watchmen of their own choice to guard their goods during the hours the Exhibition is open to the public. Appointment of such watchmen will be subject to the approval of the Director-General.

Exhibitors, or such agents as they may designate, shall be responsible for the receiving, unpacking, and arrangement of objects, as well as for their removal at the close of the Exhibition.

If products are not intended for competition, it must be so stated by the exhibitor, and they will be excluded from the examination by the International Juries.

The removal of goods will not be permitted prior to the close of the Exhibition.

Immediately after the close of the Exhibition, exhibitors shall remove their effects and complete such removal before December 31, 1876. Goods then remaining will be removed by the Director-General and sold for expenses, or otherwise disposed of, under the direction of the Commission.

Mr. John Carbutt has been appointed Superintendent of Photographic Hall, and photographers should confer with him on all matters relating to their exhibits.

Each person who becomes an exhibitor, thereby acknowledges and undertakes to keep the rules and regulations established for the government of the Exhibition.

IMPORTANT TO VISITORS.

REGULATIONS FOR ADMISSION TO THE CENTENNIAL GROUNDS DURING THE EXHIBITION.

There are thirteen places of entrance and exit, selected by reason of their proximity to main roads and the points nearest to which the railroad lines, the passenger cars, and steamboats will set down their passengers. The entrances will nearly all have four gates, one for visitors proper to the Exhibition, that is those who pay for their admission; one for persons having complimentary tickets; a third for exhibitors, representatives of the press, and employees; and a fourth for wagons. Near the entrance will be placed the exits. A number of turnstiles, varying at different points, from one to thirty-three, have been placed at the points of entrance. Of these there are, altogether, 146, and the total number of exits are 42. The thirteen points which have been selected as the locations for the exits and entrances are as follows:

No. 1, east end of Main Building; No. 2, centre of Main Building, facing Elm Avenue; No. 3, main entrance, intersection of Belmont and Elm Avenues; No. 4, centre of Machinery Hall on Elm Avenue; No. 5, on Fifty-second Street, where it intersects Fountain Avenue and Elm Avenue; No. 6, George's Hill, western entrance of Avenue of the Republic; No. 7, at the intersection of Belmont Drive and Belmont Avenue; No. 8, glen entrance on Lansdowne Drive; No. 9, Belmont Valley (entrance for visitors arriving by steamboat) or Lansdowne

MEMORANDA.

MEMORANDA.

Drive; No. 10, Horticultural Hall, entrance on Lansdowne Drive; No. 11, Lansdowne Valley (entrance for visitors by steamboat and Reading Railroad), under the bridge on Lansdowne Drive; No. 12, Memorial Hall, Lansdowne Drive, south of the former entrance; No. 13, Old River Road, at the intersection of Lansdowne Drive.

The approaches to the entrances consist of three passage ways. The visitors will enter by two of these passage ways, but the middle passage will be left clear, and a guard will be stationed near the middle of it. In case of any disturbance in the lines on either side of the middle passage, the guard will arrest the offender, draw him into the middle passage, and pass him out beyond the fences. This arrangement will tend greatly to facilitate the guard in the prompt suppression of any disturbance.

At the end of the passage will be two turnstiles, each of which will be under the control of a keeper, who will sit or stand behind a counter and receive the admission fee—a fifty-cent note—before the visitor passes the arm of the stile, which will, by a mechanical contrivance, be operated by the keeper's foot. As the stile turns it registers the entrance of the visitor at the gate, and also by electricity at the manager's office. The money when received is placed in a box under the counter, which, by a mechanical arrangement, locks itself as it is pulled from position. The box can only be opened by the bank officers.

The exits are of ingenious contrivance, and are so arranged that the turnstiles will turn *outwardly*, but not inwardly—so that a person leaving the grounds will be unable to return.

The designs of the entrances are very neat and tasteful. The entrances for vehicles being ten feet high, and necessarily wide, admit of the greatest scope for ornamentation. They are surmounted by American trophies, shields, flags, eagles, etc. A flag-staff rises at each side, and the name "International Exhibition," is over the door. The pedestrian entrances and exits are also similarly ornamented. Panels over the gates indicate whether they are for employees, etc., complimentary, or pay entrances.

ADMISSION TICKETS

TO THE CENTENNIAL GROUNDS.

The admission tickets to the Centennial grounds will be of two kinds, complimentary, and those issued to exhibitors, employees, representatives of the press, etc. In issuing complimentary tickets it is not the intention of the Centennial authorities to compliment *persons* but to recognize the offices of honor or trust which they may happen to hold. These tickets will, therefore, only be issued to *officials*. This distinction has been made because of the fact that if the Commission undertook to issue tickets to private individuals on account of their personal merit, it would be practically impossible to draw a line between those who are worthy and those who are not worthy.

The complimentary tickets will be printed on heavy note paper. The design will be, on the first page, a female figure representing America seated on a globe with a palm branch in her hand, and by her side a cornucopia. Beneath will be the words, "United States International Exhibition, Philadelphia; opening May 10; closing November 10, 1876. Complimentary." The ticket will be signed by the President of the Board of Finance, President of the Centennial Commission, and

MEMORANDA.

MEMORANDA.

Director-General. On the third page will be printed a request to the holder to deposit his card on entering, as a basis for future statistics of the Exhibition.

The tickets for exhibitors' employees, representatives of the press, etc., will be on fine card folded into two leaves. The central portion of the inner pages will be surrounded by a row of numbers corresponding with the days during which the exhibition will be open. Each day when the exhibitor enters, one of these numbers, corresponding to the date, will be punched out; and if he desires to leave the grounds during the day and return, he will receive a check which will permit him to return during that day only.

On the right inner page will be an oval space in which the holder of the ticket will be required to insert his photograph before June 1st. If the photograph is not inserted by that time the ticket will be forfeited. The tickets will not be transferable, and will be forfeited if presented by anybody else than the owner.

On the title page will be the words "International Exhibition," with the holder's name, his class, his country, and number. On the fourth page will be the words, "This ticket will not be renewed if lost."

Arrangements have been made by which the photographs of holders of tickets may be taken at a reduced rate. The tickets, which are handsomely engraved, are the work of the Philadelphia Bank Note Company.

The Centennial Photographic Company, whose studio is on Belmont Avenue, opposite the Lake, have contracted to take the photographs of exhibitors and employees for their admission tickets at fifty cents each.

CENTENNIAL NOTES.

THERE will be about 150 buildings in the Centennial grounds. The lineal number of feet of the inclosure, 16,000. Number of entrances, 13. Length of avenues and walks, seven miles. Length of horse railway, four miles.

TICKETS OF ADMISSION.—The regular admission ticket will be a *United States Fifty-Cent Note.* Visitors can prepare themselves with these admission tickets before coming, and so avoid confusion, or they can be procured at the Ticket Offices near the entrances.

THE CENTENNIAL FOUNTAIN is located on Fountain Avenue, near Machinery Hall. It was erected by the Catholic Total Abstinence Union of America. It consists of a circular basin 40 feet in diameter, in the centre of which is a mass of rock, surmounted by a statue of Moses 15 feet high; the whole height being 35 feet. Extending from the main platform, in the shape of a Maltese Cross, are four arms, each terminating in a platform, upon which is a drinking fountain, surmounted by a statue 9 feet high. Sculptor, Herman Kern, Philadelphia. Cost, $50,000.

A BEAUTIFUL FOUNTAIN is situated between the Main Building and Machinery Hall.

AMONG *the prominent Statues which adorn the grounds are the following:*

THE STATUE OF COLUMBUS, erected by the Italians of Philadelphia, will be situated at the junction of Fountain and Belmont Avenues. It is to be unveiled on the Fourth of July.

MEMORANDA.

MEMORANDA.

THE STATUE OF RELIGIOUS LIBERTY consists of two figures representing Liberty protecting Religion. It is being erected by the B'nai B'rith Hebrew order. The pedestal and statue stand 20 feet in height. Cost, $30,000. Sculptor, Mr. Ezekiel, of Richmond, Va. Executed in Rome.

STATUE OF WILLIAM PENN.—This is the Colossal Bronze intended for the New Public Buildings at Broad and Market Streets. Sculptor, Bailey.

STATUE OF JOHN WITHERSPOON, one of the signers of the Declaration of Independence, and an eminent divine, is in bronze, also modeled by Bailey, and stands on a pedestal of Quincy granite. It is situated on the slope east of the Art Gallery. It is 35 feet in height, and was erected by the Presbyterian denomination in honor of the Centennial.

EMANCIPATION.—This is a group in marble, executed by Miss Harriet Hosmer, the American sculptor, in Rome. It is intended to commemorate the emancipation of the slaves in this country, and consists of a colossal female figure representing Freedom, lifting a child representing the negro race, from the earth, or from a condition of slavery. This group will probably be placed in the Women's Pavilion, as a specimen of women's work, as Miss Hosmer applied early for space to exhibit it there.

THE MEMORIAL MONUMENT, which is to be placed in New York harbor to commemorate the friendship which has always existed between France and the United States, will be placed in the Centennial grounds during the Exhibition. It will be situated on the border of the lake north of Machinery Hall. It is 48 feet high, and from it electric lights will illuminate the grounds at night. The monument is the work of M. Bartholdi, of Paris.

THE SAWYER OBSERVATORY is situated on Belmont Hill, outside the Centennial grounds. It is 185 feet high, and commands an elevation of over 400 feet above the Schuylkill River. It is fitted with a fine elevator, capable of carrying 40 persons, and 125 can be accommodated on the landing place at the top. The view from this lofty elevation is truly magnificent.

HOTEL CHARGES.—Let no one be kept away from the Exhibition by reports of extortionate charges, for the restaurant prices in the grounds are regulated by the Centennial Commission, and are the same as charged outside, while the highest priced hotels have fixed their charges at $5.00 per day, which will be adhered to during the season, and other houses run from this down to $1.50 per day. Lodging and meals can also be had separately and at low rates.

EXTRA.

N. P. A. CONVENTION FOR 1876.

Just as this work is about going to press, I learn that the Executive Committee have held a meeting, and decided to call a Convention of the N. P. A. on August 15th, 16th, and 17th. This settles the question of the Centennial Convention of the National Photographic Association, and it is to be hoped that every member will determine to come, and make it one of the most successful and profitable meetings we have ever had.

There will be no expense for a hall, as the Director-General has kindly granted the use of the hall in the Judges' Pavilion for the purpose. The Photographic Exhibit will be already in order; and as all photographers, as well as everybody else, will want to visit the great Exhibition, they can make their arrangements to come at the time above stated, and show to the world that the National Photographic Association of the United States is a living and wide-awake institution.

116

North Seventh Street,

OFFICE OF

The Philadelphia Photographer.

PHOTOGRAPHIC PUBLICATIONS.

WILSON'S LANTERN JOURNEYS,
WAYMOUTH'S VIGNETTE PAPERS,
IMPROVED PHOTOGRAPH COVERS,
HERMAGIS CELEBRATED LENSES.

GIHON'S CUT-OUTS, GIHON'S OPAQUE,
GLASS STEREOGRAPHS, STEREOSCOPES,
MAGIC LANTERNS, LANTERN SLIDES,
PRIZE PICTURES (three series),

CENTENNIAL VIEWS,
THE ROBINSON TRIMMER, ROBINSON GUIDES.

FOR SALE BY

BENERMAN & WILSON,

116 North Seventh St., Philadelphia.

SCOVILL

Manufacturing Company,

MANUFACTURERS AND IMPORTERS OF

Photographic Materials

OF EVERY DESCRIPTION,

FOR THE DEALER,
    FOR THE PHOTOGRAPHER,
        FOR THE AMATEUR.

MANUFACTURERS OF THE

American Optical Company's Apparatus.

SOLE AGENTS FOR

Samuel Peck & Co.'s Goods,

AND

PHENIX FERROTYPE PLATES.

FACTORIES: { Waterbury, Conn., New Haven, Conn., New York City.

Warerooms, 419 & 421 Broome St., New York.

MAGIC LANTERNS
AND
LANTERN SLIDES.

We make a specialty of Slides, and keep in stock the largest assortment in America, of the best French and English make.

OUR STOCK OF
CENTENNIAL SLIDES

Is especially rich, comprising, as it does, all the best things of the Exhibition. Exhibitors will find these very taking.

By special concession of the *Centennial Photographic Company*, we have secured the exclusive use of their negatives, and these slides can be had only of us.

$100 OUTFITS.

An improved Sciopticon and 116 beautiful Slides for one hundred dollars. This cannot be beaten. With our immense stock we can offer the most favorable terms, and purchasers will find it to their advantage to consult us before buying.

WILSON'S LANTERN JOURNEYS.

This Lecture-Book should be in the hands of every exhibitor. It contains six journeys, and gives a graphic description of **600 places and things** in all parts of the world.

THE MAGIC LANTERN.

A monthly journal devoted to the interests of those who love and use the Lantern.

Four Catalogues mailed on receipt of twenty-five cents.

BENERMAN & WILSON,
116 North Seventh St., Philadelphia.

PHOTOGRAPHIC PUBLICATIONS FOR 1876.

The following are our leading publications, which are indispensable in every gallery where progress and a high order of work is desired:

The Philadelphia Photographer,

THE BEST PHOTOGRAPHIC MAGAZINE PUBLISHED,

And the only one embellished with a beautiful photograph in each number.

PRICE, $5.00 PER YEAR.

PROF. VOGEL'S HAND-BOOK OF PHOTOGRAPHY.
Second Edition. Price, 3.50.

BIGELOW'S ALBUM OF LIGHTING AND POSING.
Price, $6.00.

THE PRACTICAL PRINTER.
A Complete Guide. Price, $2.50.

PROF. VOGEL'S POCKET REFERENCE-BOOK.
Price, $1.50.

BURNET'S HINTS ON COMPOSITION.
Price, $3.50.

THE PHOTOGRAPHER TO HIS PATRONS.
Price by the thousand.

THE FERROTYPER'S GUIDE.
Price, 75 cents.

CENTENNIAL PHOTOGRAPHIC DIARY.
Price, 75 cents.

Published by

BENERMAN & WILSON,
116 N. Seventh St., Philadelphia.

John G. Hood. Established **1865**. Wm. D. H. Wilson.

WILSON, HOOD & CO.,

DEALERS IN

Photographic Goods,

FRAMES,

Stereoscopes, and Views.

BY APPOINTMENT,

WHOLESALE AND RETAIL AGENTS

FOR THE SALE OF THE PUBLICATIONS OF THE

Centennial Photographic Co.

SALESROOMS,

No. 822 Arch Street,

PHILADELPHIA, PA.

Burnisher or Planisher,

MANUFACTURED UNDER AN

EXCLUSIVE LICENSE

GRANTED BY

W. E. LOCKWOOD, Assignee of J. F. SCHUYLER,

WHOSE PATENT BEARS DATE

February 24, 1863. Reissued June 1, 1875.

PRICE LIST.

6-inch Roll, $20.	14-inch Roll, $40.
10-inch Roll, $30.	18-inch Roll, $50.

Also, 30-inch Roll, for hand or steam-power (this machine is especially adapted for large work). Price $300.

CAUTION.

The suit of J. P. BASS, assignee of E. R. WESTON v. PECK, tried in the United States Circuit Court, at Portland, Maine, October 8th, 1875, the JURY in rendering a verdict for the defendant found:

1.—That Weston, assignor to Bass, was not the original and first inventor of a burnishing machine by which a surface is given to the article to be burnished, by feeding it under pressure over the surface of a burnishing tool.

2.—That he was not the original and first inventor of the combination of a burnishing tool and a friction feed-roll.

3.—That he was not the original and first inventor of the combination of the feed-roll and adjustable burnishing tool.

The evidence on which the jury based this finding was that relating to the invention and use by the late J. F. Schuyler of a machine by which a surface was given to the article to be burnished by feeding it under pressure over the surface of a burnisher, rendered stationary, the paper being fed over said burnisher by means of a friction feed-roll.

The patent of W. E. Lockwood, assignee of John F. Schuyler, dated February 24th, 1863, was issued June 1st, 1875,

WITH THE FOLLOWING CLAIMS!

1.—**As an improvement in the art of Planishing paper, submitting the paper to friction under pressure between a roughened feed roller and a Planisher, substantially as described.**

2.—**The combination in a Paper Planishing Machine, of a Planisher with a draw-filed roller, for controlling the paper while it is under pressure between the said roller and planisher, all substantially as set forth.**

To Photographers and Dealers in Photographic Goods:

Whatever doubts may have existed in the minds of photographers as to the merits of the controversy between the undersigned, W. G. Entrekin, and the owners of the Weston' Patents for Burnishers, will be set at rest by the perusal of the above claims, by the verdict of the jury declaring the *patent of Weston to be invalid.*

While the undersigned feels disposed to treat with liberality, photographers who have been induced by threatening circulars to purchase the Weston and other machines that infringe the above claims, he will hold them responsible as infringers of the above-mentioned re-issued patents of William E. Lockwood in the use of said machines without first paying the small license fee which is now demanded.

On the other hand, the most prompt and determined legal measures will be taken against those infringers who deliberately, and after being thus duly cautioned, make, use, or sell burnishing machines in which is embodied the invention claimed in the said re-issued patent.

W. G. ENTREKIN, *Sole Licensee,*
Under grant by WM. E. LOCKWOOD, *Patentee*

Manayunk, Philada., April 25, 1876.

SHERMAN & CO.,

PRINTERS,

Seventh and Cherry Sts.,

PHILADELPHIA.

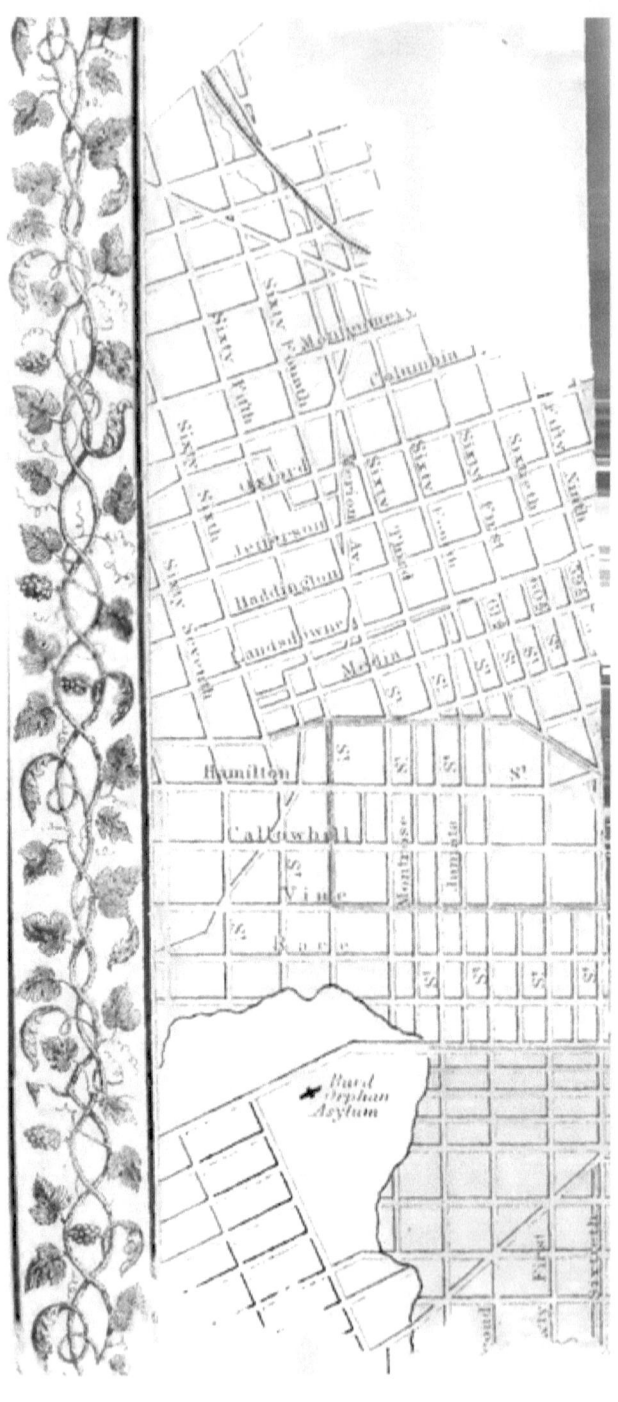

www.ingramcontent.com/pod-product-compliance
Lightning Source LLC
Chambersburg PA
CBHW020146170426
43199CB00010B/903